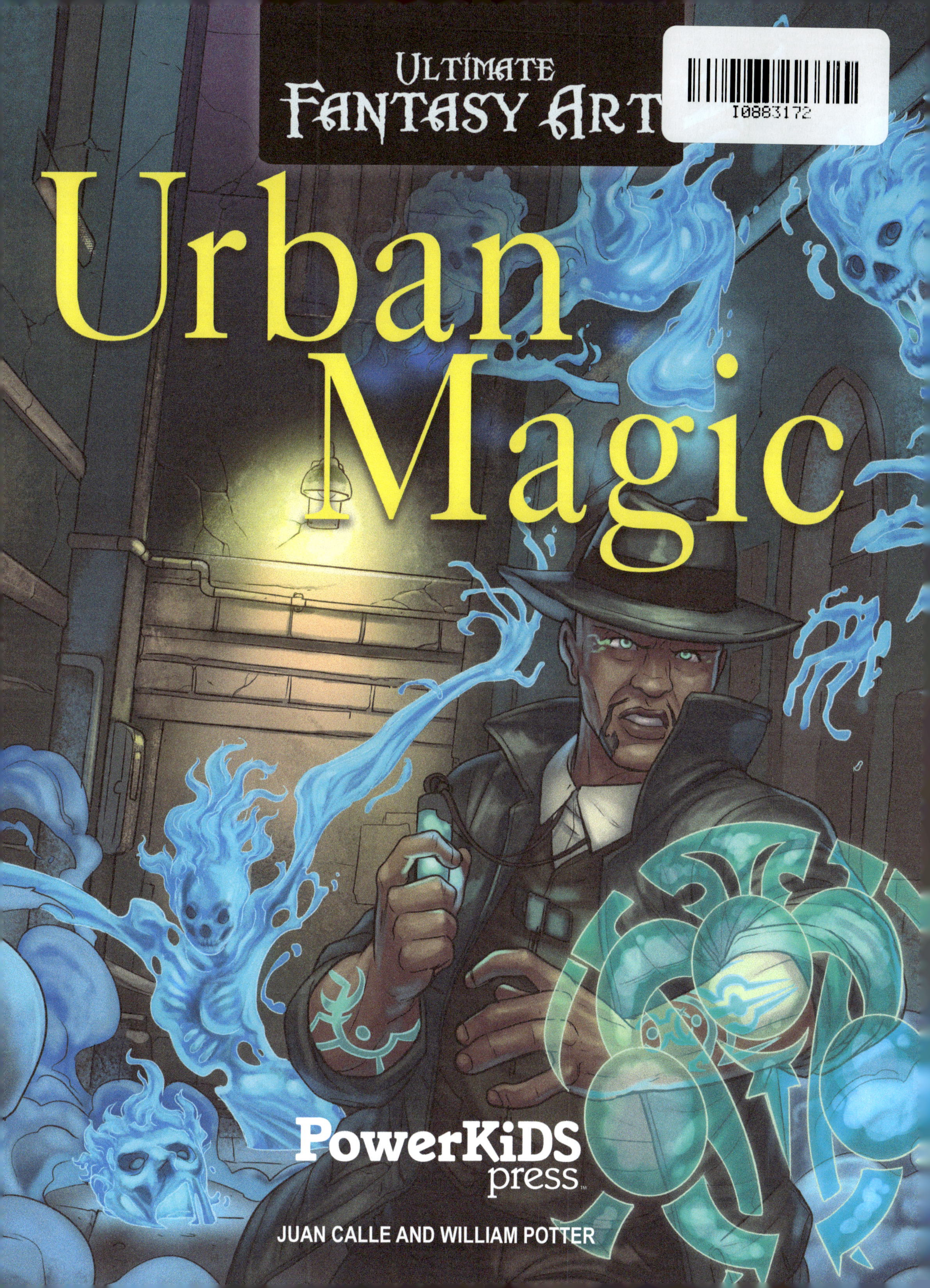
ULTIMATE FANTASY ART
Urban Magic
PowerKiDS press
JUAN CALLE AND WILLIAM POTTER

Published in 2020 by **The Rosen Publishing Group, Inc.**
29 East 21st Street, New York, NY 10010

Cataloging-in-Publication Data

Names: Calle, Juan. | Potter, William.
Title: Urban magic / Juan Calle and William Potter.
Description: New York : PowerKids Press, 2020. | Series: Ultimate fantasy art | Includes glossary and index.
Identifiers: ISBN 9781725303348 (pbk.) | ISBN 9781725303362 (library bound) | ISBN 9781725303355 (6pack)
Subjects: LCSH: Fantasy in art--Juvenile literature. | Drawing--Technique--Juvenile literature.
Classification: LCC NC825.F25 C355 2020 | DDC 741.2--dc23

Manufactured in the United States of America

CPSIA Compliance Information: Batch CSPK19: For Further Information contact Rosen Publishing, New York, New York at 1-800-237-9932.

CONTENTS

FANTASY COMES TO LIFE!

Welcome to the world of fantasy! From sewer dwellers to paranormal detectives, you'll find lots of urban magic in this book.

All you need to get started is a pencil and paper, but here are a few more tools you can use to add some extra magic.

Pencils come in various hardnesses—H for hard, B for soft. A 2H pencil is good for making light marks that don't smudge, and 2B for adding softer finishes for feathers, fur, and smoke. Try different hardnesses to find those you're most comfortable with. You'll also need a sharpener and eraser.

Collect pictures to inspire you. Models and figurines are also useful as reference for drawing your own fantasy folk.

Any paper will do for drawing on, especially for early sketches and planning. If you use water-based paints, you may want to use a thicker paper that absorbs the paint without it spreading—or bleeding—across the surface.

You can use a waterproof ink pen to go over your pencil lines before painting. Alternatively, use a nib pen or a fine brush dipped in ink. Using a brush and ink requires some patience and a steady hand but can produce impressive results.

For the finished picture use a range of brushes with water-based or acrylic paints, plus a tray or plate to mix different shades.

While many fantasy lands are full of forests, craggy mountains, and crumbling ruins, you may still need to use a ruler as a guide for straight weapons, buildings, mechanical devices, and planning the perspective of an action scene.

PERSPECTIVE AND PALETTES

A little knowledge of 3-D shapes and perspective goes a long way in helping the most incredible scene look real.

You can use these 3-D shapes as the building blocks for more complicated and natural forms, such as this spiked mace.

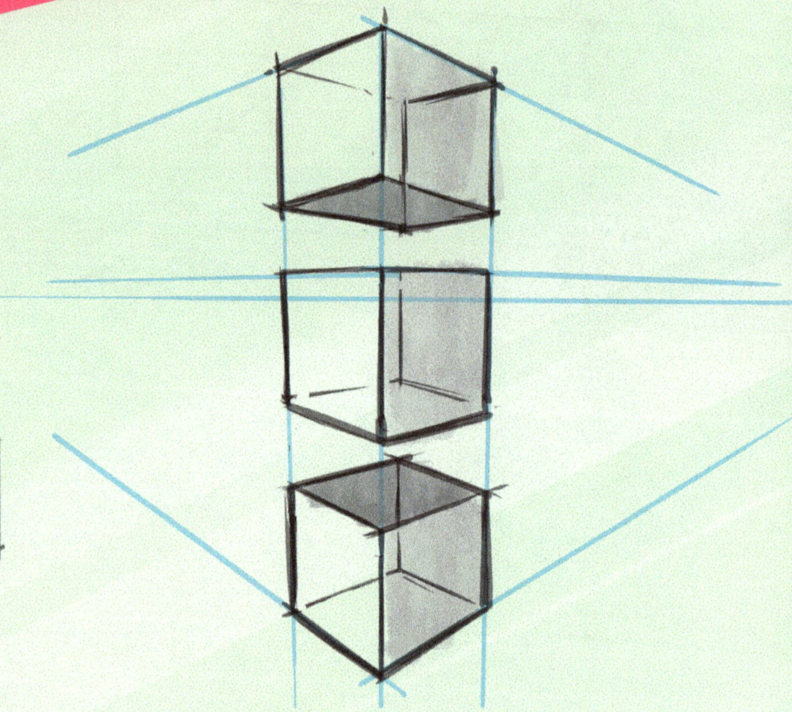

Now, look at these blocks seen from an angle. Opposite sides appear closer together the farther away they get. These perspective lines continue until they join at a vanishing point.

And here's a wall, getting smaller in the distance, following its own perspective lines. The guards also appear smaller in the distance, following the same rules.

Perspective lines are useful when you're building a scene that includes buildings and depth.

Reds suggest blood, fire, and passion. Use these to raise the temperature of your fantasy scenes, when monsters use their flaming breath or evil spirits arise from dark domains.

Browns and greens are calming, reminding you of nature. Many adventures involve quests across countrysides. Create drama by beginning a journey in a relaxing green environment and transitioning to a more threatening domain of red and black.

Blues are cooler. They suggest frosty, unfeeling, ghostly moods. Use these for moonlit scenes and the chilly castles of vampires.

UNDERGROUND MAGIC

Mystics and magical beings exist in our midst. They hide their presence with cunning spells, while waging a war between light and dark. Who might you conjure up?

SHAPE-SHIFTER STYLE

Mid-transformation, the shape-shifter is half male, half female, but the eyes suggest her true form is something totally different. The eyes are lizard-like, matching her chameleon-like powers of camouflage. She smiles confidently, knowing she can hide as whomever she likes.

SHAPE-SHIFTER

Your supernatural beings may be hiding in full sight, in disguise, or as a shape-shifter. Is this a man, a woman, or something else entirely? As a female agent, the shape-shifter stole the heart of a trusting senator to gain his passwords. Now she will take his place and steal his secrets, too.

BLIND SEER

Appearances can deceive in the world of urban fantasy. Play with expectations. For example, this man is blind but can perceive much more than the average person. His special sight allows him to see beyond the physical plane. He senses the supernatural beings that cross into our world and can predict the fate of those he touches.

BLIND SEER STYLE

Despite his age, the blind seer appears strong and carries great wisdom. He does not use touch to figure out his surroundings as he already knows what is ahead. His clothes are simple and loose-fitting, hiding a lean, powerful physique gained from years of martial arts practice.

UNDERGROUND MAGIC *continued*

SEWER DWELLER STYLE

The creature from the sewer is like a wild animal in human form, dressed in stolen rags. His hair is thinning, and his teeth, fingers, and toenails are long, like claws. Though he seems extremely unhealthy, he is strong and quick. He is also wary, trying to work out if the viewer is friend, foe, or feast.

SEWER DWELLER

Where might your supernatural creatures hide in the city? This sewer dweller is as pale as the moonlight, having never seen the sun. He has spent his life living in tunnels below the streets, surviving on the scraps that float downstream or the vermin that share his underground home.

ASSASSIN STYLE

Voiceless and without fear, this creature from the dark lives only on the orders of his master. His body is lean as he has no need for food. His clothes are dark to help him hide in the night. His daggers are razor sharp and leave wounds that cannot be healed by mortal hands.

MINDLESS ASSASSIN

When supernatural beings need to deal with their urban enemies, who do they send? This silent assassin is a servant of one dark lord. His single purpose—to seek and destroy his target. He is the perfect killing machine, sticking to the shadows, then launching his attack without a whisper.

PARANORMAL DETECTIVE

With expert knowledge of the world's many dark arts, the paranormal detective is available for hire, to solve magical mysteries and free those in need from hauntings and curses.

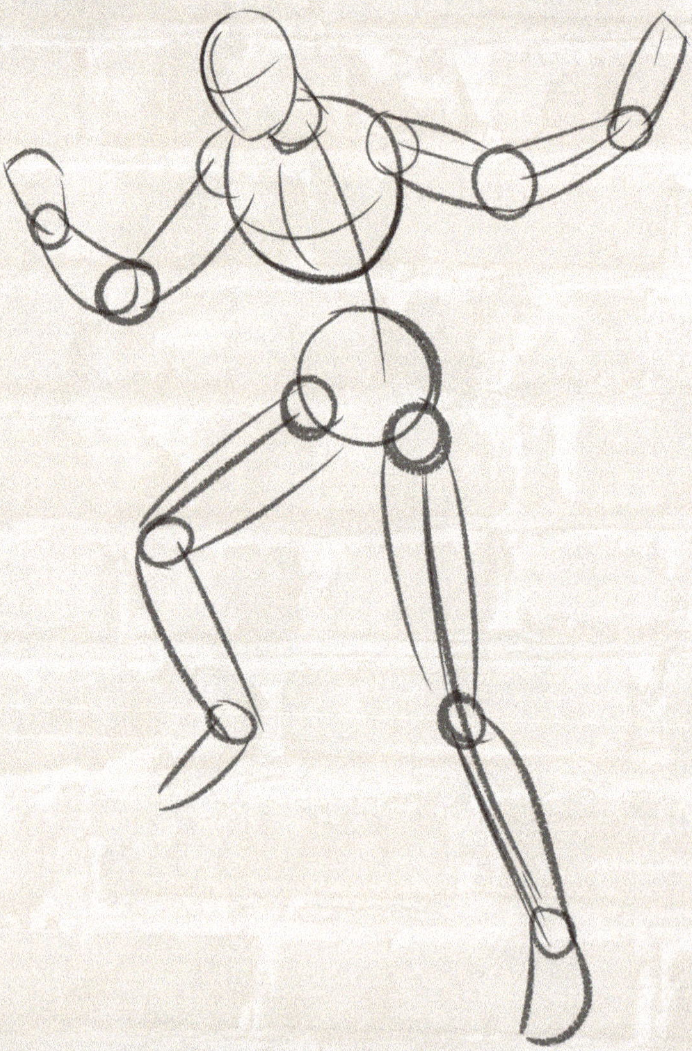

1. STICK FIGURE

Using light pencil marks, draw a few simple lines to sketch the pose of the detective with one hand in a fist, the other shaping a mystic shield.

2. JOINTED FIGURE

Now, fill out his figure with 3-D shapes. Draw a cross on the face to indicate the line of the eyes and nose. Use circles to mark the position of joints.

3. CLOTHING

Now dress the figure, giving the detective a brimmed hat, an open overcoat, and a protective amulet swinging around his neck.

4. FINISHED PENCILS

In the finished pencils, creases from the figure's clothing curve away from his joints and around his waist. He has magical tattoos on both arms, and is drawing a similar glowing symbol in midair.

TOP TIP

Magical symbols you can use in your urban fantasy adventures include stars, eyes, skulls, crosses, and ancient-looking letters. Place these on protective brooches and tattoos, or use them for wall and floor paintings used for protection or for luring spirits to Earth.

5. PALETTE

Paint the supernatural detective's clothes in subdued leathery browns, contrasting with the bright glowing blue of the mystic symbols and amulet.

6. FINAL ART

In the finished painting, the detective is lit by the cool shades of his mystic symbol. His tattoos and eyes also glow with this supernatural light.

SECRET SABOTEUR

With her face hidden by a mask, the saboteur strikes against the enemies of freedom. Her identity is hidden to protect her family, or to hide a face scarred through tragedy.

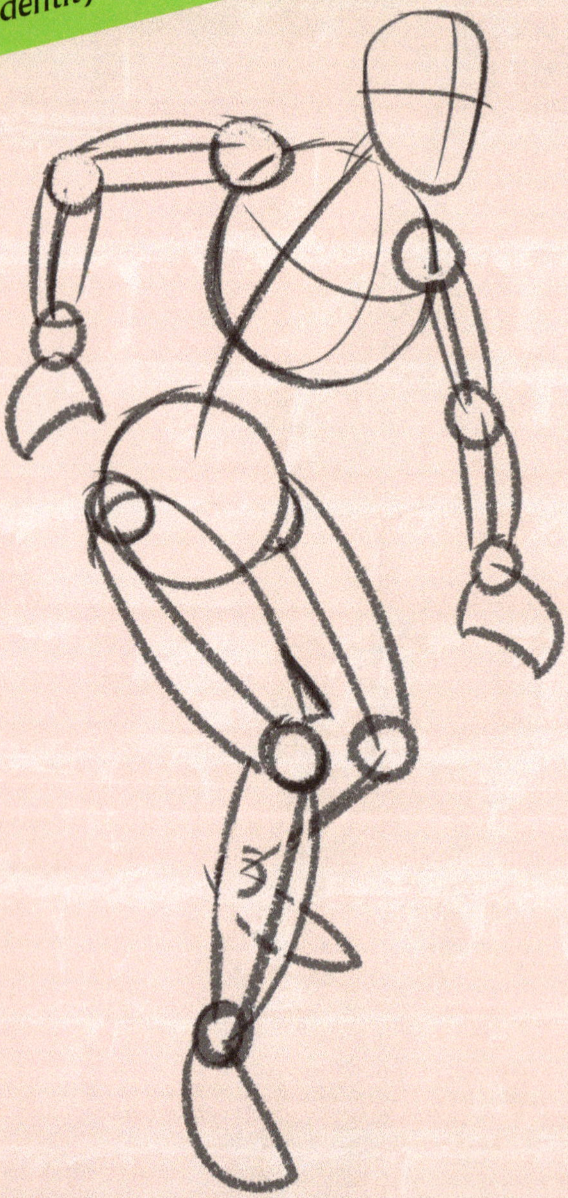

1. POSE

Using light pencil marks, draw a few lines for the pose of the saboteur, with a twist in the upper body. She crouches slightly, and holds her equipment bag with her right hand.

2. FIGURE WORK

Now, fill out her figure. She is light and slim—ideal for sneaking into buildings—but her protective clothes and tools add bulk.

3. PALETTE

Choose stealthy dark blues and greens for the saboteur's outfit. Her clothes are military issue with straps and Kevlar protection. The mask and goggles conceal most of her face.

4. FINAL ART

In the finished art, the saboteur is mostly in shade, just as she likes. Only her protective padding, goggles, and clips reflect the little light there is.

CREATURE SUMMONED

The monster has been summoned from the dark side by unholy rituals, but will it obey the demands of those that called it, or devour them?

1. ROUGH FIGURE

Using light pencil marks, draw a few simple lines to outline the monster. The creature is stepping through a portal from a dark world. Use circles for the head, chest, and pelvis. Add tentacles from its head, and bat-like wings from its shoulders.

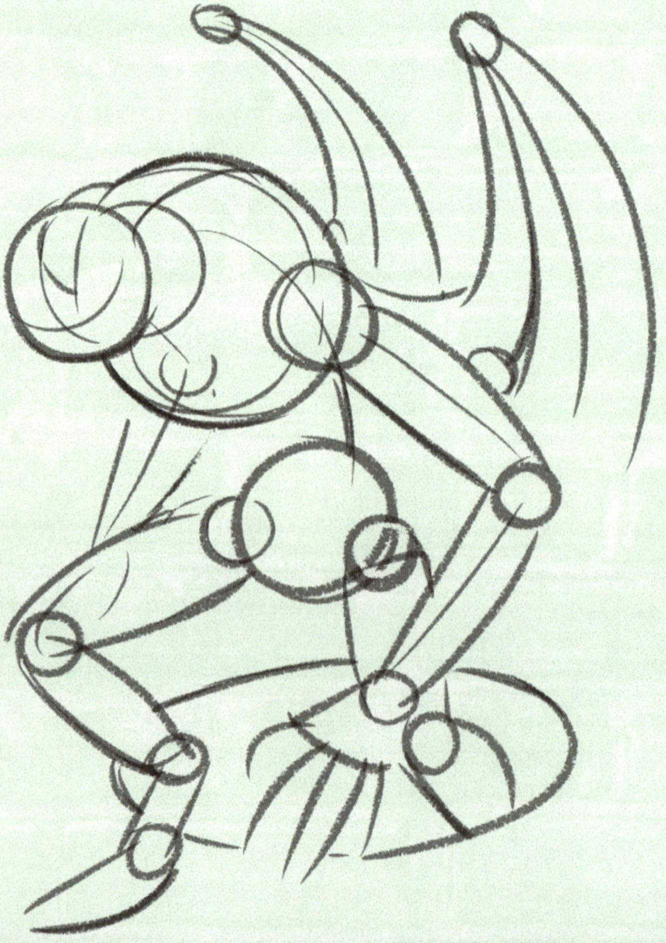

2. JOINTED BODY

Now, fill out the figure with 3-D shapes. The creature is in a crouched position. The wings curve up above the head. Use circles to mark the position of joints, including an extra one in the long foot.

3. ANATOMY

Now, add more mixed monster bodywork. The creature's head tentacles hang like a beard of snakes around its round mouth. A tall, bony fin rises over the shoulders. The fingers and toes are long and clawed.

4. GRUESOME DETAILS

Go to town on the gruesome details. The monster's limbs have a rough finish. There are large warty growths over the shoulders. Its small jaw is filled with needle-sharp teeth. Add candles and wisps of smoke around the portal.

CREATURE SUMMONED *continued*

5. PALETTE

The monster is painted in unnatural shades of blue, with purple-pink areas of flesh around the head and ribs. The warty growths are an unhealthy green.

6. FINAL ART

In the finished picture, the creature emerges from an unknown realm through a cloud of smoke. Highlights have been added to the skin to give it an aged, wrinkly finish, and the tentacles glisten like those of a squid.

WARLOCK'S WHEELS

This street warlock arrives in style. His flame-painted motorcycle gets a lot of attention and gets him out of trouble. Here's how to build an awesome bike for an urban wizard.

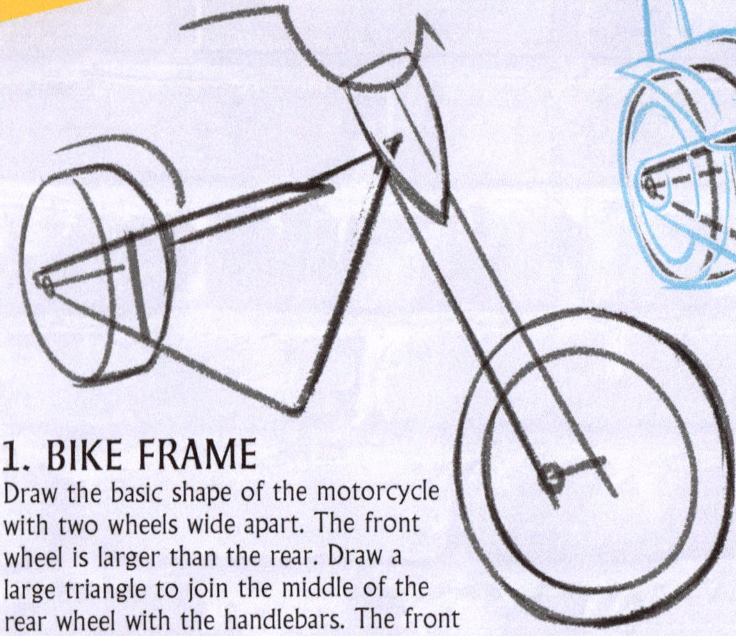

1. BIKE FRAME

Draw the basic shape of the motorcycle with two wheels wide apart. The front wheel is larger than the rear. Draw a large triangle to join the middle of the rear wheel with the handlebars. The front wheel is joined by long front forks to the handlebars.

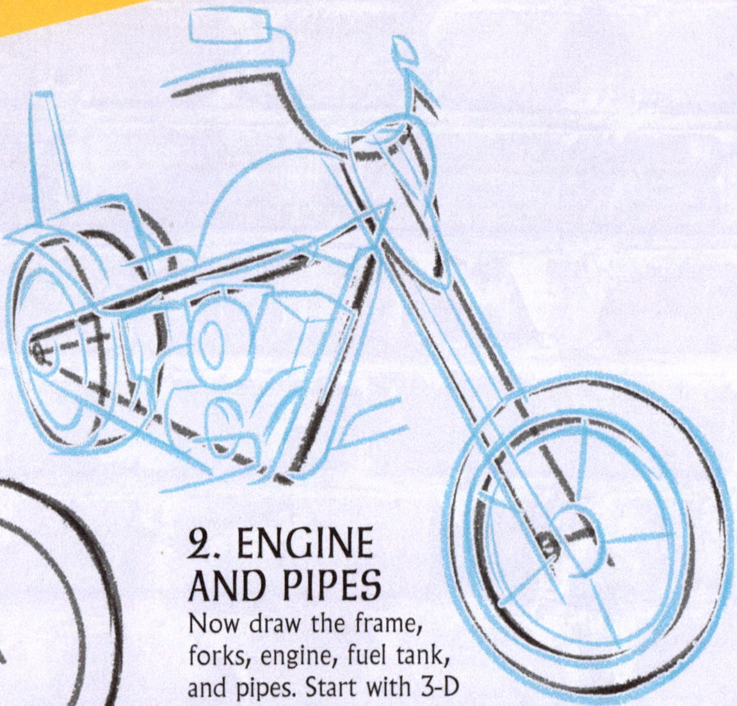

2. ENGINE AND PIPES

Now draw the frame, forks, engine, fuel tank, and pipes. Start with 3-D shapes—blocks and cylinders—then add the curves and mechanical detail.

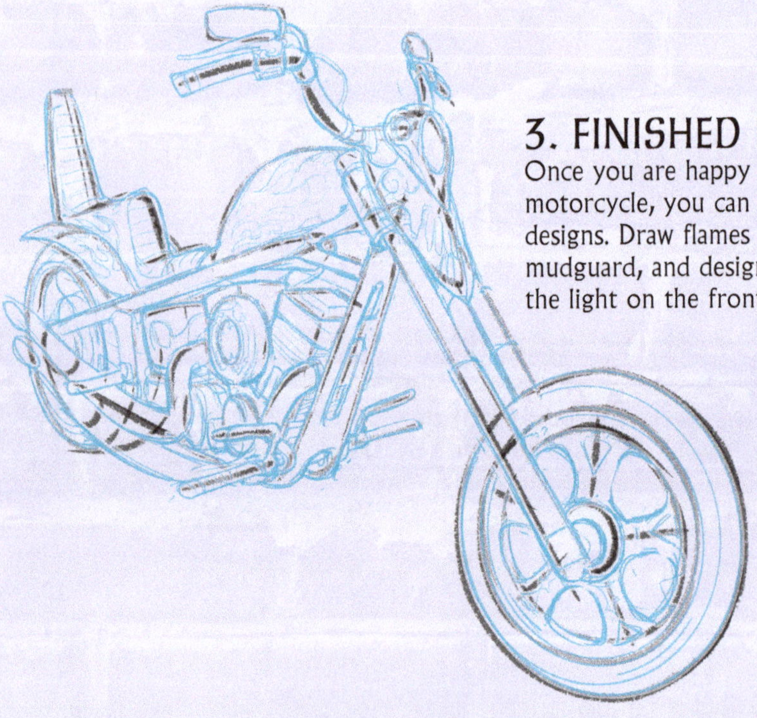

3. FINISHED PENCILS

Once you are happy with the build of the motorcycle, you can add the warlock's custom designs. Draw flames on the tanks and rear mudguard, and design a skull-like frame for the light on the front forks.

4. PALETTE

The painted parts of the motorcycle are red and orange while the metal parts are shiny chrome, painted using light stripes for reflections.

5. FINAL ART

The finished motorcycle looks very flashy. The red and orange of the painted flames makes the motorcycle appear to be on fire—perfect for a wizard at war with supernatural forces. While intimidating, it also suggests its owner is a bit of a show-off.

NOT WHAT IT SEEMS

Look carefully for clues that magic is afoot. Here are some details you can add to a scene to suggest that supernatural forces are close by.

Though disguised, this paranormal being cannot fully hide his snake-like, forked tongue and pointed ears. Could he also be hiding horns beneath his top hat?

Animals may be spirit creatures, or acting as the eyes of supernatural beings. This cat's red eyes are a giveaway, and look extra scary when they peer out from the darkness.

Strange symbols painted on a wall may not mean anything to you, but they could be a message for unearthly eyes.

A bizarre shadow is cast, but there is no visible figure causing it. Its shape is clearly not human.

CAPTURING NATURE

Knowing how to draw natural features will be useful, whether your story takes place in a real or imaginary world. Here are some tips on drawing natural features.

RUNNING WATER

For a stream of running water, use a soft pencil to indicate the direction of the water flow around obstacles. Draw dark patches following the flow, where a person, tree, or building is reflected in the water.

TREES

Draw a curving trunk with branches spreading from about head height. You can leave the branches bare if it's a winter scene, or add cloud shapes for leafy bushes covering the ends of the branches in summer.

ROCKS

Pile up several 3-D shapes to build a rocky formation. Round off the shapes, then add dots and cracks over the surface for texture.

SUPERNATURAL STRIKE

In an abandoned subway station, spectral forces have found a route into our world. The occult detective and saboteur need all their knowledge of the dark arts and tech to force them back.

1. Plan the scene in a rough sketch. The occult heroes are racing forward alongside the subway track while fighting off the winged attackers.

2. Use perspective lines to build up the scene, with the tunnel and track stretching from a point in the middle of the page. The whole image is tilted at a dramatic angle.

3. In the finished pencils, the winged monsters are dark in tone. The scene is lit from the right by the motorcycle's headlight. Eerie graffiti has been added to the tunnel walls. Is it meant as a warning?

4. The subway is gloomy and forboding, painted with brown shades, with the monsters in darker tones. The only bright shades are those on the detective's flashy motorcycle, a mystic shield, and the wall paintings.

SUPERNATURAL STRIKE *continued*

The finished, painted scene is action-packed, with spells and smoke canisters expelling clouds of gas to confuse the army of winged beasts.

GLOSSARY

3-D Three-dimensional, which means having length, breadth, and depth.

anatomy The human body.

camouflage Hidden using disguise.

highlight The white area that helps to make a drawing look solid and draw attention to its shape.

mace A heavy club used as a weapon.

occult To do with the supernatural.

palette The range of shades chosen by an artist.

perspective The representation on a flat surface of a three-dimensional image as seen by the eye, to give the illusion of distance and depth.

portal A door or entrance.

saboteur Someone who practices sabotage, or deliberate damage to something.

seer Someone who can predict the future.

shape-shifter A mythical figure who can take the form of an animal.

supernatural Belonging to an existence outside the visible world.

tech Short for "technology."

vanishing point The point at which parallel lines seem to meet in the distance.

warlock A male sorcerer, or wizard.

FURTHER INFORMATION

Books

Alexander, Rob, and Finlay Cowan and Kevin Walker. *The Compendium of Fantasy Art Techniques*. Hauppauge, NY: Barron's, 2014.

Blando, Jared. *How to Draw Fantasy Art and RPG Maps*. Cincinnati, OH: Impact Books, 2015.

Cook, Trevor, and Lisa Miles. *Drawing Fantasy Figures.* New York, NY: Gareth Stevens Publishing, 2011.

Websites

Art for Kids Hub

www.artforkidshub.com/how-to-draw

This website has instructions for drawing all sorts of things.

How to Draw a Monster

www.drawingforall.net/how-to-draw-a-monster/

Follow the steps on this page to draw a monster.

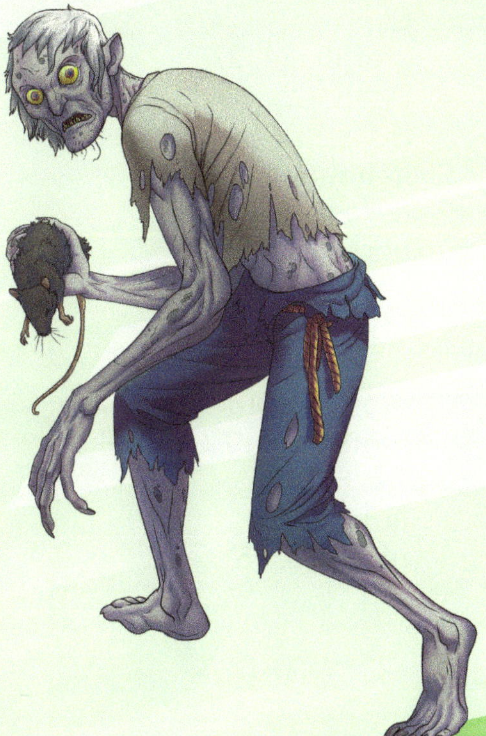

Publisher's note to educators and parents: Our editors have carefully reviewed these websites to ensure that they are suitable for students. Many websites change frequently, however, and we cannot guarantee that a site's future contents will continue to meet our high standards of quality and educational value. Be advised that students should be closely supervised whenever they access the Internet.

INDEX